The Future of Learning at Work:
How Technology, Neuroscience and Personalization will Shape the Workforce

Frederique Bergeron

Copyright © 2024 Frederique Bergeron

All rights reserved.

ISBN: 9798340482037

CONTENTS

1	The Learning Revolution	4
2	The Science of Learning: What Neuroscience Tells Us	9
3	The Rise of Adaptive Learning Platforms	15
4	AI and Machine Learning: Transforming Training Programs	21
5	Microlearning and Just-in-Time Learning	27
6	Personalized Learning Journeys for Every Employee	33
7	Building a Culture of Continuous Learning	39
8	Reskilling and Upskilling for the Future	46
9	Learning Beyond Borders: Global Trends and Remote Work	53
10	What's Next? Future Trends in Workplace Learning	60

INTRODUCTION: LEARNING IN A TIME OF TRANSFORMATION

The world of work is changing at a pace we've never seen before. Technological advancements like artificial intelligence, machine learning, and automation are transforming industries at their core, while demographic shifts—such as the rise of millennials and Gen Z in the workforce—are pushing organizations to rethink how they operate. At the same time, the COVID-19 pandemic accelerated remote and hybrid work, making clear that the traditional office-based model is no longer the only path forward. These shifts have reshaped how we think about work, but more importantly, how we think about learning and development in the workplace.

In this new era, the old methods of employee training—often characterized by one-size-fits-all approaches, static e-learning modules, or sporadic, one-off workshops—are no longer enough. The need for continuous learning, delivered in real-time and personalized to each individual's role and growth trajectory, has never been more critical. Organizations are being forced to adapt, or they risk falling behind in a hyper-competitive, rapidly evolving market.

The Workforce is Evolving—Are Learning Methods Keeping Up?

Today's workforce is diverse, not just in terms of demographics but also in learning preferences. Employees expect to have control over their learning journeys. They want access to relevant, on-demand learning resources that are not only aligned with their career goals but also tailored to their individual strengths and weaknesses. The workforce is now multi-generational, with employees spanning from Boomers to Gen Z. This demographic mix means that companies must cater to a wide range of needs, from those who may be of a digital-first generation, comfortable with AI-driven platforms, to those who are more accustomed to traditional, in-person training methods.

Additionally, the gig economy and the rise of project-based work have altered expectations for development. Workers today may not stay at one organization for decades, as previous generations did. Instead, they are more likely to take on short-term roles or freelance gigs, which means they seek continuous learning that can travel with them throughout their careers. This creates a demand for portable, scalable learning solutions that provide real-world skills and credentials they can apply regardless of where they work.

Why Continuous Learning is No Longer Optional

The half-life of skills is shrinking. According to some estimates, technical skills now become outdated in as little as five years. Jobs that didn't exist a decade ago—like AI specialists, data scientists, and social media managers—are now in high demand, while others are disappearing due to automation. Companies that fail to reskill or upskill their workforce are not just at risk of falling behind but becoming obsolete.

To remain competitive, businesses must foster a culture of continuous learning. This isn't just about offering employees opportunities to develop new skills, but about embedding learning into the fabric of everyday work. Continuous learning means moving beyond the annual training session or compliance module. It means creating learning ecosystems where employees have access to real-time information, adaptive learning platforms, and mentorship opportunities—all designed to help them grow on a day-to-day basis.

Why Traditional Approaches Are Failing

For years, many organizations relied on classroom-style learning or static e-learning platforms to train their employees. These methods, while useful in their time, are no longer adequate in a world where change is constant and immediate. Traditional training often takes employees away from their work for extended periods, making it difficult to apply what they learn in real-time. Worse, it can often be too generic, providing little relevance to an employee's specific role or development needs.

In contrast, today's employees want learning to be integrated into their work. They want tools that help them upskill on the job, whether through microlearning—bite-sized learning modules that can be accessed on the go—or adaptive platforms that adjust to their individual progress and needs. And they want to see immediate value. If learning is seen as disconnected from their day-to-day tasks, motivation dwindles, and the investment in development falls flat.

The Urgency of Transformation

The rapid pace of technological change is creating urgency for organizations to rethink how they approach learning and development. It's no longer just about staying relevant; it's about survival. Organizations that adopt continuous learning strategies, incorporating new technologies like AI-driven learning platforms or virtual reality simulations, will be able to keep pace with the speed of change. Those that don't will be left behind, struggling to meet the demands of both their workforce and the marketplace.

It's also important to recognize that learning isn't just about hard skills. The future workforce will need soft skills like emotional intelligence, adaptability, and creative problem-solving. As automation takes over routine tasks, human-centric skills will become more critical. These are the skills that machines can't replicate but are essential for navigating complex, unpredictable challenges. The organizations that succeed will be those that can foster both technical expertise and human skills through holistic learning programs.

What Lies Ahead

This book will explore how organizations can rise to the challenge of this transformation. We'll dive into the cutting-edge tools that are shaping the future of learning, from AI and adaptive platforms to microlearning and just-in-time learning. We'll look at the science behind how people learn best and how organizations can foster environments where learning is embedded into the workflow, rather than an afterthought. We'll explore case studies from companies leading the way in employee development, and we'll offer actionable strategies for how you can transform learning in your own organization.

The future of work demands a new kind of learner and a new kind of workplace. The companies that thrive will be those that build continuous learning ecosystems—where employees are equipped with the tools, knowledge, and mindsets they need to adapt, grow, and lead in the face of constant change.

1 THE LEARNING REVOLUTION

The End of the Traditional Learning Model

For decades, the traditional model of workplace learning remained largely unchanged. Employees were brought into a room—either physically or virtually—and walked through a set curriculum. Training was delivered in a one-size-fits-all approach, often separated from the day-to-day work environment. In the early 2000s, online learning platforms gained traction, offering more flexibility in when and where employees could access training materials. But even then, the underlying philosophy was the same: learning was something done periodically, often in isolated bursts.

However, the static approach to learning is no longer sufficient. The rapid pace of technological change, combined with the increased complexity of work, has disrupted this traditional model. Employees are no longer just looking to "learn once and apply forever." Instead, they need continuous access to new knowledge and skills to keep up with ever-evolving demands. This shift is not just about new tools or delivery methods; it's about a complete revolution in how we think about learning in the workplace.

From Learning Events to Learning Ecosystems

The most significant shift in this revolution is the move from isolated "learning events" to integrated "learning ecosystems." A learning event is a one-time experience—like a workshop, seminar, or training session—designed to teach a specific skill or concept. These events may be valuable in the short term, but their impact often fades quickly because they are not tied to the learner's ongoing work.

A learning ecosystem, on the other hand, is a dynamic environment that fosters continuous learning over time. In this model, learning is not a separate event but an integral part of the daily workflow. Employees have access to resources, tools, and support systems that enable them to learn as they work. The most forward-thinking organizations are shifting toward this model because it allows for personalized, on-demand learning that directly addresses the skills employees need in real time.

The Role of Technology in the Learning Revolution

Technology has been one of the primary drivers of the learning revolution. New tools and platforms are making it easier than ever to deliver personalized, scalable learning experiences. Here are some of the key technological advancements that are transforming workplace learning:

1. **Adaptive Learning Platforms**:
   Adaptive learning uses artificial intelligence (AI) and machine learning algorithms to deliver personalized learning experiences. These platforms analyze individual learners' progress, strengths, and weaknesses and adjust the learning content in real-time to meet their specific needs. Unlike traditional e-learning, where everyone follows the same path, adaptive learning tailors each person's journey, ensuring that learners spend more time on areas they need to develop and less on concepts they have already mastered. This not only boosts engagement but also improves retention and application of knowledge.

2. **Microlearning**:
   Microlearning breaks down complex subjects into bite-sized, easily digestible modules that can be completed in a few minutes. These small learning units fit seamlessly into an employee's daily routine, allowing them to learn incrementally without being taken away from their primary tasks for extended periods. Microlearning is particularly effective in today's fast-paced work environments, where employees often struggle to carve out time for long training sessions. By focusing on a single concept or skill in each module, microlearning maximizes retention while minimizing disruption to the workflow.

3. **Mobile Learning**:
   As more employees work remotely or on the go, mobile learning has become a key component of the learning revolution. Modern learning platforms are designed to be accessed from any device, at any time, giving employees the flexibility to learn when and where it's most convenient for them. Whether they're commuting, working from home, or traveling for business, mobile learning ensures that development opportunities are always within reach. This flexibility is particularly valuable in global organizations with dispersed teams across time zones.

4. **Gamification**:
   Gamification incorporates game mechanics—such as points, levels, leaderboards, and rewards—into learning programs to increase motivation and engagement. By turning learning into a competitive or goal-oriented activity, gamification taps into people's natural drive to achieve and improve. Gamified learning experiences are often more

interactive and engaging than traditional training methods, helping to reinforce learning through active participation.

5. **Social and Collaborative Learning**:
   Modern learning platforms are also incorporating social learning elements, allowing employees to learn from each other through peer interactions, forums, and knowledge-sharing communities. Collaborative learning encourages employees to share their experiences, ask questions, and provide feedback to one another. This peer-to-peer learning creates a sense of community and reinforces the idea that learning is an ongoing, collective process.

6. **Virtual Reality (VR) and Augmented Reality (AR)**:
   Though still emerging, VR and AR are poised to transform workplace learning by offering immersive, hands-on experiences in a virtual environment. VR can simulate real-world scenarios that employees might encounter on the job—whether it's a sales pitch, customer service interaction, or even a hazardous situation in industries like manufacturing or healthcare. These immersive simulations allow employees to practice skills in a controlled, safe environment before applying them in the real world. AR, meanwhile, can overlay digital information onto the physical world, providing on-the-job guidance and real-time learning support.

The Learning Experience Platform (LXP)

In the past, many companies relied on Learning Management Systems (LMS) to deliver training content. While LMS platforms are still widely used, they are increasingly being supplemented or replaced by Learning Experience Platforms (LXP). Unlike LMS, which are primarily designed for managing and tracking compliance training, LXPs are designed to deliver personalized, learner-centric experiences.

An LXP allows employees to choose their learning paths based on their interests and career goals, much like a Netflix-style recommendation system. These platforms integrate formal training content with informal learning opportunities, such as articles, podcasts, and videos, creating a more engaging and flexible learning environment. LXPs also foster social learning by encouraging employees to share content and collaborate on learning experiences. As a result, LXPs are driving the shift toward continuous, self-directed learning.

From Compliance to Competence

A critical aspect of the learning revolution is the shift from compliance-based learning to competence-based learning. For many years, workplace training was seen primarily as a way to meet regulatory requirements—whether it's health and safety training, compliance with industry standards, or mandatory certifications. While these are still important, the focus is shifting toward building real competence and capability.

Competence-based learning is about ensuring that employees are not just checking boxes but are genuinely mastering the skills and knowledge they need to perform at a high level. This involves a more personalized approach to learning, where employees have access to ongoing development opportunities that align with their roles and career aspirations. Companies are now focusing on measuring and assessing competence in a way that goes beyond traditional metrics like attendance and course completion, looking instead at how effectively employees can apply what they've learned in their everyday work.

The Business Case for the Learning Revolution

The learning revolution is not just about improving employee engagement or retention—it's a business imperative. Companies that embrace continuous learning are better equipped to adapt to change, innovate, and stay ahead of the competition. They are more agile and resilient in the face of market disruptions, and they can attract top talent by offering meaningful development opportunities.

Studies consistently show that organizations with strong learning cultures outperform their peers. A study by Bersin by Deloitte found that companies with high-impact learning cultures were 92% more likely to innovate, 46% more likely to be first to market, and had 37% greater employee productivity. These companies also reported higher levels of employee engagement and retention. In today's knowledge-driven economy, learning is a key driver of business success.

Conclusion: Embracing the Revolution

The learning revolution is well underway, and it's reshaping how organizations approach employee development. To stay competitive, companies must move beyond outdated models of learning and embrace new technologies, strategies, and mindsets that prioritize continuous, personalized learning. The future of work will belong to organizations that can foster a culture of lifelong learning, where employees are empowered to grow, adapt, and thrive in an ever-changing world.

In the following chapters, we'll dive deeper into the technologies, tools, and strategies that are driving this revolution. From adaptive learning platforms to the neuroscience of learning, we'll explore how organizations can build learning ecosystems that meet the demands of the future workforce.

2 THE SCIENCE OF LEARNING: WHAT NEUROSCIENCE TELLS US

In the past decade, our understanding of how people learn has been profoundly influenced by advances in neuroscience. While traditional learning theories focused largely on external factors—such as instructional design or environmental conditions—modern neuroscience reveals that the most important learning processes happen inside the brain. By understanding how the brain works, organizations can create more effective learning environments that foster deeper learning, improve retention, and accelerate skill development.

This chapter explores the key insights from neuroscience that are shaping the future of learning and how organizations can apply these insights to transform their employee development programs. From neuroplasticity and memory formation to the role of motivation and emotion in learning, we'll delve into the science behind how people learn best and how organizations can leverage these principles to create a culture of continuous learning.

Neuroplasticity: The Brain's Ability to Learn and Adapt

At the core of learning is a concept called **neuroplasticity**—the brain's ability to reorganize itself by forming new neural connections. Neuroplasticity allows the brain to adapt to new experiences, environments, and information, which is why people can learn and grow throughout their lives. Unlike the old belief that the brain was fixed after childhood, we now know that adults can continue to build new skills and knowledge through targeted learning efforts.

The more we engage with new information or practice a skill, the stronger the neural pathways associated with that information or skill become. This is why repetition and practice are essential to mastering any task. Learning isn't a one-time event—it's a process of building and reinforcing connections in the brain. Understanding this helps organizations design training programs that allow for consistent practice and reinforcement rather than isolated, one-time learning sessions.

Practical Applications of Neuroplasticity in Workplace Learning:

- **Continuous Learning**: Because neuroplasticity relies on repetition and reinforcement, organizations should create learning programs that encourage continuous learning. This can be done through microlearning modules, follow-up activities, or on-the-job practice.

- **Spaced Learning**: Neuroscience suggests that learning is more effective when spaced out over time rather than condensed into a single event. Employees benefit from repeated exposure to the material over weeks or months, rather than cramming all the content into a few days.

- **Reflection and Application**: Encourage employees to reflect on what they've learned and apply it in real-world situations. Application strengthens the neural connections and embeds the learning more deeply.

Memory Retention: How the Brain Stores Information

Memory plays a central role in learning, as it allows individuals to retain and recall information over time. Neuroscientists have discovered that memory retention is not a simple, linear process. Instead, the brain sorts through information and decides what to store in long-term memory based on factors like emotional significance, repetition, and relevance.

There are two main types of memory that are important for workplace learning: **short-term (or working) memory** and **long-term memory**. Short-term memory holds information temporarily, but unless that information is transferred to long-term memory, it is quickly forgotten. For learning to be truly effective, organizations must focus on strategies that help transfer new knowledge into long-term memory, where it can be retrieved when needed.

Practical Applications for Memory Retention:

- **Chunking Information**: The brain can only hold a limited amount of information in short-term memory at any given time. By breaking complex information into smaller, manageable "chunks," learners can more easily process and store it in long-term memory.

- **The Spacing Effect**: Information is better retained when learning is spaced out over time. Rather than delivering large amounts of content in one go, organizations can break learning into smaller sessions with time intervals in between, giving the brain time to consolidate the information.

- **Active Recall and Testing**: Encouraging employees to actively recall information through quizzes or flashcards helps strengthen memory. Testing is not just a way to evaluate learning—it's a method of learning itself, as it forces the brain to retrieve and strengthen neural pathways.

Motivation and Emotion in Learning

The role of motivation in learning cannot be overstated. Neuroscience tells us that motivation is closely linked to dopamine, a neurotransmitter that drives feelings of pleasure and reward. When people are motivated, their brains release dopamine, which not only makes learning more enjoyable but also enhances memory retention. Motivation, in essence, primes the brain for learning.

Similarly, **emotion** plays a critical role in how people learn and retain information. Research shows that emotionally charged experiences are more likely to be remembered because they activate the amygdala, the brain's center for emotional processing. This is why experiences that evoke emotion—whether positive or negative—tend to leave a lasting impact.

Practical Applications for Motivation and Emotion:

- **Intrinsic vs. Extrinsic Motivation**: While extrinsic rewards (such as bonuses or promotions) can motivate employees to learn, intrinsic motivation (the desire to learn for personal growth and satisfaction) is more powerful. Organizations should create learning environments that tap into employees' intrinsic motivations, such as opportunities for mastery, autonomy, and purpose.

- **Creating Emotional Connections**: Make learning experiences more engaging by incorporating storytelling, real-world examples, and interactive elements. When employees feel an emotional connection to the material, they are more likely to remember and apply what they've learned.

- **Gamification**: One way to increase motivation is by incorporating game elements into learning programs. Points, badges, leaderboards, and rewards can stimulate dopamine release and create a sense of achievement, making learning more enjoyable and reinforcing engagement.

The Importance of Sleep and Rest in Learning

Another critical insight from neuroscience is the importance of sleep in learning and memory consolidation. When we sleep, the brain processes the information we've encountered during the day, consolidating it into long-term memory. Sleep also clears out toxins that accumulate in the brain, allowing for better cognitive function and learning the next day.

In addition to sleep, taking breaks during learning sessions has been shown to improve retention. The brain needs time to rest and process new information, which is why long, uninterrupted training sessions are often less effective than shorter sessions with breaks.

Practical Applications for Sleep and Rest:

- **Encourage Healthy Sleep Habits**: Organizations can promote the importance of sleep by offering flexible work schedules that allow employees to prioritize rest. This not only improves learning outcomes but also boosts overall productivity.

- **Incorporate Breaks in Learning Programs**: Learning sessions should include regular breaks to give the brain time to rest and consolidate information. Encourage employees to step away from their desks and recharge, even during intense periods of learning.

Attention and Focus: The Brain's Limited Resources

One of the biggest challenges to learning in today's world is the constant barrage of distractions. Neuroscience tells us that attention is a limited resource, and the brain can only focus on one thing at a time. Multitasking is a myth—what we are actually doing when we "multitask" is rapidly switching between tasks, which diminishes the brain's ability to deeply process information.

To create an environment conducive to learning, it's essential to minimize distractions and encourage focused attention. This is especially important in a digital age where notifications, emails, and social media compete for our mental bandwidth.

Practical Applications for Focus and Attention:

- **Single-Tasking**: Encourage employees to focus on one task at a time, especially during learning sessions. Design learning programs that allow employees to engage deeply with the material, free from distractions.

- **Eliminate Digital Distractions**: When designing online learning experiences, minimize potential distractions such as pop-ups or multiple tabs. Consider using full-screen modes for e-learning platforms and encouraging employees to turn off notifications during training.

- **Mindfulness and Focus Training**: Some organizations have begun incorporating mindfulness practices into their learning programs.

Techniques like meditation or breathing exercises can help employees improve focus and reduce stress, which in turn enhances learning outcomes.

Social Learning and the Brain

Humans are inherently social beings, and our brains are wired for connection. Neuroscience shows that social interactions play a critical role in learning. When we engage with others, our brains release oxytocin, a hormone that promotes bonding and trust. This social connection enhances learning by making the experience more engaging and emotionally resonant.

Additionally, social learning leverages the concept of **mirror neurons**, which are brain cells that fire both when we perform an action and when we observe someone else performing the same action. This is why we can learn by watching others, and why collaborative learning environments—where employees learn from their peers—are so effective.

Practical Applications for Social Learning:

- **Peer Learning**: Encourage peer-to-peer learning by creating opportunities for employees to collaborate and share knowledge. This can be done through group projects, mentorship programs, or social learning platforms that facilitate interaction.

- **Learning Communities**: Build learning communities where employees can engage in discussions, share best practices, and ask questions. The more employees interact with each other during the learning process, the more likely they are to retain and apply what they've learned.

- **Storytelling and Role-Playing**: Use storytelling and role-playing exercises to create emotional connections and simulate real-world scenarios. These methods engage mirror neurons and help employees practice new skills in a safe, supportive environment.

Conclusion: Applying Neuroscience to Workplace Learning

The science of learning tells us that effective workplace training goes far beyond delivering content. It's about understanding how the brain processes, retains, and applies new information—and designing learning experiences that align with these principles. By leveraging insights from neuroscience, organizations can create more engaging, effective, and personalized learning environments that empower employees to thrive.

A real-world example of this can be seen in how Volvo applied neuroscience principles to transform its corporate learning programs:

Case Study: Volvo's Use of Neuroscience to Transform Learning[1]

Overview:
Volvo recognized a need to evolve its learning and development practices, as the previous approach focused on the number of training days rather than the quality of learning. With most courses relying on PowerPoint presentations and lacking follow-up or reinforcement, Volvo sought to create more effective, engaging learning experiences.

Solution:
Volvo partnered with Stella Collins of Stella Learning to apply neuroscience-based principles in their training. They focused on helping trainers understand how learning works and shifted from traditional methods to using tools such as pictures, videos, and contextual training. The new approach emphasized making learning more interactive and engaging, especially for engineers and technicians, by incorporating brain-friendly techniques.

Results:
Volvo saw significant improvements in engagement and efficiency. A new "YouTube"-style video series generated 9,000 additional learning touchpoints, providing just-in-time learning that helped technicians perform better. The adoption of neuroscience-driven learning techniques also resulted in substantial cost savings, including £3 million by replacing a planned retraining program with a short video.

In the following chapters, we'll explore how to integrate these neuroscience principles into modern learning platforms and programs, and how organizations can harness the power of adaptive learning, gamification, and social learning to build a culture of continuous growth and development.

Endnotes

1. Chartered Institute of Personnel and Development (2014). *Neuroscience in action Applying insight to L&D practice.* Engaging Learners at Volvo. neuroscience-action_2014-applying-insight-ld-practice_tcm18-9714.pdf (cipd.org)

3 THE RISE OF ADAPTIVE LEARNING PLATFORMS

In today's rapidly evolving work environment, the concept of one-size-fits-all learning is quickly becoming obsolete. As organizations face increasing demands to reskill and upskill employees, traditional learning methods—where every employee follows the same path—fail to meet the diverse needs of a modern workforce. This is where **adaptive learning platforms** come into play, revolutionizing how organizations deliver personalized learning experiences to their employees.

Adaptive learning uses technology, data, and artificial intelligence (AI) to tailor learning experiences to the individual needs, skills, and knowledge gaps of each employee. These platforms analyze a learner's performance in real time, adjusting content, pace, and even the level of difficulty to optimize learning outcomes. Instead of a rigid, linear approach, adaptive learning creates a fluid, dynamic experience that evolves as the learner progresses.

In this chapter, we'll explore how adaptive learning platforms work, why they are transforming corporate learning, and how organizations can leverage these systems to improve engagement, retention, and performance.

What is Adaptive Learning?

At its core, adaptive learning is a personalized approach to education and training that adjusts the learning path based on the needs of the learner. Unlike traditional training programs, where all employees receive the same content in the same order, adaptive learning platforms continuously assess an individual's progress and adapt accordingly.

For example, if an employee excels in a particular topic, the platform might skip over related content or present more advanced material. Conversely, if an employee struggles with a concept, the platform will adjust by providing additional resources, practice exercises, or simpler explanations. This personalized approach ensures that each learner gets exactly what they need, when they need it, to be successful.

Adaptive learning platforms typically use AI and machine learning algorithms to:

- Assess learner performance in real time
- Identify strengths and weaknesses
- Tailor content based on individual needs

- Adjust pacing and difficulty to maximize engagement
- Provide immediate feedback to reinforce learning

The Benefits of Adaptive Learning in the Workplace

1. **Personalization at Scale**

One of the most significant advantages of adaptive learning platforms is their ability to deliver personalized learning at scale. In a large organization, employees come from diverse backgrounds, with varying levels of experience, knowledge, and skill. A generic training program often fails to address these differences, leading to disengagement or frustration. With adaptive learning, every employee receives a unique learning path tailored to their specific needs, making the experience more relevant and impactful.

For example, in a compliance training program, an experienced employee might breeze through the basics but require more in-depth learning on new regulations. Meanwhile, a newer employee might need to spend more time mastering foundational concepts. Adaptive learning platforms automatically make these adjustments, ensuring that each employee gets the right amount of training without wasting time on material they already know.

2. **Increased Engagement and Retention**

One of the biggest challenges in workplace learning is keeping employees engaged. Traditional training programs often follow a one-size-fits-all approach that can lead to boredom or overwhelm, depending on the learner's prior knowledge. Adaptive learning platforms solve this problem by delivering content that is always at the right level of challenge for each individual, keeping them in a state of **flow**—the optimal zone where they are neither bored nor overwhelmed.

This heightened engagement leads to better retention of information. By presenting content that is directly relevant to each learner's needs and goals, adaptive learning platforms make it easier for employees to stay focused and motivated throughout the training process. Furthermore, the real-time feedback provided by these platforms helps learners see their progress, reinforcing a sense of accomplishment and driving further engagement.

3. **Efficiency and Time Savings**

In a fast-paced work environment, time is a valuable resource. Traditional training methods often require employees to spend unnecessary time on material they already know or don't need. Adaptive learning platforms address this inefficiency by allowing employees to skip content they've already mastered and focus on areas where they need improvement.

By streamlining the learning process and eliminating redundant training, adaptive learning platforms reduce the time employees spend in training, allowing them to get back to their jobs more quickly. This makes learning more efficient for the organization and less disruptive to the flow of work.

4. **Immediate Feedback and Continuous Improvement**

Feedback is critical to the learning process, but in traditional training programs, feedback is often delayed or generic. Adaptive learning platforms provide immediate, personalized feedback based on each learner's performance. This allows employees to understand their mistakes in real time and correct them before moving forward.

The continuous nature of adaptive learning also encourages ongoing improvement. As employees progress through the learning material, the platform adjusts the content to challenge them further, ensuring that learning doesn't stop after the initial training session. This leads to a deeper mastery of skills and concepts over time, supporting long-term employee development.

5. **Data-Driven Insights for Organizations**

Adaptive learning platforms don't just benefit employees; they also provide valuable data and insights for organizations. These platforms track learner performance, progress, and engagement in real time, giving HR and L&D teams a clear picture of each employee's learning journey.

This data allows organizations to:

- Identify knowledge gaps across the workforce
- Assess the effectiveness of training programs
- Make data-driven decisions about employee development
- Customize learning interventions for underperforming teams or individuals
- Predict future learning needs based on trends in performance data

With this level of insight, organizations can optimize their learning and development strategies to better align with business goals and improve overall performance.

How Adaptive Learning Platforms Work

Adaptive learning platforms use a combination of AI, machine learning, and data analytics to personalize the learning experience. Here's a closer look at the process:

1. **Assessment**: The platform typically begins by assessing the learner's current knowledge and skills. This might involve a pre-test, a diagnostic quiz, or a review of previous learning data. The goal is to establish a baseline understanding of where the learner stands.

2. **Personalization**: Based on the assessment, the platform tailors the learning experience to the individual's needs. The content, difficulty level, and pacing are all adjusted to create a customized learning path. If a learner performs well on a particular topic, they might move ahead quickly; if they struggle, the platform provides additional support and resources.

3. **Real-Time Adaptation**: As the learner progresses, the platform continuously adapts based on their performance. If the learner encounters difficulty, the system might slow down, offer easier material, or present the information in a different format (e.g., video, text, or interactive simulations). Conversely, if the learner excels, the platform introduces more challenging content to keep them engaged.

4. **Feedback and Reinforcement**: Throughout the learning process, the platform provides real-time feedback, helping learners understand their mistakes and reinforcing correct behaviour. This immediate feedback is essential for ensuring that learners stay on track and build confidence as they progress.

5. **Data Collection**: Every interaction with the platform is tracked, allowing the system to learn more about the learner's strengths, weaknesses, and preferences. This data is then used to further personalize the learning experience and provide valuable insights to the organization.

Real-World Applications of Adaptive Learning

Many industries are already leveraging adaptive learning platforms to improve employee development. Here are a few examples:

1. **Corporate Training**: Companies like IBM and Accenture use adaptive learning to deliver personalized training experiences to their employees. IBM's AI-powered learning platform, Watson, tailors

content based on individual needs, while Accenture's platform uses data-driven insights to match employees with learning opportunities that align with their career goals.

2. **Healthcare**: In the healthcare industry, adaptive learning platforms are being used to train doctors, nurses, and other medical professionals. These platforms allow healthcare workers to stay up-to-date with the latest medical procedures and protocols, while also providing personalized learning experiences based on their specialties and areas of need.

3. **Sales Training**: Adaptive learning is particularly useful in sales training, where employees often come from diverse backgrounds and have varying levels of experience. Platforms like MindTickle use adaptive learning to tailor sales training content to each individual's strengths and weaknesses, helping them develop the specific skills they need to succeed.

4. **Compliance Training**: Compliance training is often seen as a necessary but dull part of corporate life. Adaptive learning platforms can make compliance training more engaging by personalizing the content to the learner's role and experience level. This ensures that employees get relevant, actionable information, rather than generic training that doesn't apply to their specific context.

The Future of Adaptive Learning

As AI and machine learning technologies continue to evolve, the potential for adaptive learning platforms will only grow. In the future, we can expect even more sophisticated systems that not only personalize learning content but also predict future learning needs based on individual performance and industry trends.

For organizations, this means the ability to create truly personalized learning journeys that adapt to each employee's career path, ensuring that they are always equipped with the skills and knowledge they need to succeed. As these platforms become more widespread, adaptive learning will likely become the standard for corporate training, replacing traditional, static learning models with a dynamic, data-driven approach.

Conclusion: Embracing Adaptive Learning for the Future

Adaptive learning platforms represent a significant leap forward in how organizations approach employee development. By delivering personalized, data-driven learning experiences, these platforms can help companies upskill their workforce more efficiently and effectively. As we move into an era where continuous learning is essential for success, adaptive learning platforms offer a powerful tool for organizations looking to stay ahead of the curve.

4 AI AND MACHINE LEARNING: TRANSFORMING TRAINING PROGRAMS

The use of artificial intelligence (AI) and machine learning (ML) in training programs is no longer a futuristic concept—it's happening right now, transforming the way employees learn and develop new skills. AI and ML are revolutionizing corporate training by creating more personalized, data-driven, and efficient learning experiences. From predictive analytics to tailored content delivery, these technologies enable organizations to meet the diverse needs of their workforce while improving engagement, retention, and performance.

In this chapter, we'll explore how AI and machine learning are reshaping workplace training, how organizations can leverage these technologies, and the real-world benefits they offer to both employees and businesses.

What Are AI and Machine Learning in the Context of Training?

Before diving into their applications, let's clarify what we mean by AI and machine learning in the context of training.

- **Artificial Intelligence (AI)** refers to the simulation of human intelligence by machines. In training programs, AI can automate tasks such as content curation, learner assessments, and even coaching. AI systems can learn from data and make decisions, allowing them to deliver more personalized learning experiences.

- **Machine Learning (ML)** is a subset of AI that involves the use of algorithms to identify patterns in data and make predictions or decisions without being explicitly programmed. In training, ML can help identify learning gaps, predict future performance, and recommend tailored learning paths based on an individual's progress and behaviours.

Together, AI and ML make it possible to offer truly personalized, adaptive learning experiences that evolve with the learner, allowing organizations to train employees more effectively and efficiently than ever before.

How AI and Machine Learning Are Transforming Corporate Training

1. **Predictive Analytics for Personalized Learning**

One of the most powerful applications of AI and machine learning in training is predictive analytics. Using vast amounts of data, these systems can predict how employees will perform on certain tasks, identify knowledge gaps, and recommend personalized learning paths to close those gaps. By analyzing patterns in employee behaviour, AI can determine which skills or knowledge areas need reinforcement and suggest relevant content or activities.

For example, if an employee consistently struggles with a particular concept, the AI system can recommend additional resources, such as articles, videos, or quizzes, to help them improve. Conversely, if the system detects that the employee is excelling in certain areas, it might suggest more advanced material to keep them challenged and engaged.

This data-driven approach ensures that employees receive the most relevant training for their needs, maximizing learning efficiency and improving overall performance.

2. **Content Curation and Delivery**

Traditional training programs often rely on static content that is the same for every learner. AI and machine learning, however, allow for dynamic content curation and delivery, tailoring learning experiences to each individual. These systems can pull from a vast library of resources—such as videos, articles, case studies, and quizzes—and assemble them into a personalized learning path based on the learner's role, experience, and progress.

For instance, an AI-powered training platform can curate content that aligns with an employee's career goals or interests, making the learning experience more relevant and engaging. As the employee progresses through the training, the platform continuously updates the content to reflect their needs, ensuring that they are always receiving the most appropriate material.

This type of tailored content delivery not only keeps learners engaged but also ensures that they spend their time on topics that matter most to their development.

3. **Automated Assessments and Feedback**

AI and machine learning are also transforming how organizations assess employee learning. Instead of relying solely on traditional exams or quizzes, AI-powered platforms can evaluate learners in real time by tracking their interactions with the training material. These platforms use advanced algorithms to assess how well employees are grasping concepts and provide immediate feedback to help them improve.

For example, AI systems can analyze how long it takes a learner to answer a question or how often they revisit certain material. Based on this data, the system can adjust the difficulty level of future content or provide targeted feedback to help the learner overcome specific challenges.

This real-time assessment and feedback process allows employees to course-correct as they learn, leading to better knowledge retention and skill development. It also reduces the burden on managers and HR professionals, who no longer need to manually grade or assess every piece of training.

4. Chatbots and Virtual Coaches

Another key innovation driven by AI in corporate training is the rise of chatbots and virtual coaches. These AI-powered assistants are available 24/7 to answer employee questions, provide guidance, and even deliver mini-lessons on specific topics. Chatbots can interact with learners through text or voice, offering a personalized, conversational experience that feels more like a one-on-one coaching session than a traditional classroom setting.

Virtual coaches can guide employees through training programs, offering encouragement, answering questions, and suggesting additional learning resources when needed. This creates a more engaging, interactive learning environment where employees can receive real-time support without having to wait for a human instructor.

For example, if an employee is stuck on a particular lesson, they can ask the chatbot for clarification. The AI system might provide a brief explanation, point them to relevant resources, or even ask follow-up questions to assess their understanding.

This type of AI-driven support helps employees stay on track and ensures that they get the help they need when they need it.

5. Improving Engagement and Reducing Training Fatigue

One of the biggest challenges in corporate training is keeping employees engaged. Traditional, one-size-fits-all programs can quickly lead to training fatigue, where learners become bored or overwhelmed by irrelevant material. AI and machine learning address this problem by personalizing the learning experience to match the learner's pace, preferences, and knowledge level.

By delivering content that is neither too easy nor too difficult, AI-driven platforms keep employees in the **flow state**—the zone where they are fully engaged and focused. These platforms also use gamification elements, such as points, badges, and leaderboards, to motivate learners and make the training experience more enjoyable.

Furthermore, AI systems can monitor engagement levels and adjust the learning experience accordingly. If the system detects that a learner is disengaged—perhaps because they are spending too little time on the material or repeatedly skipping content—it can introduce more interactive elements or adjust the pacing to re-engage the learner.

6. Continuous Learning and Upskilling

AI and machine learning are enabling organizations to shift from static, one-off training sessions to continuous learning environments. Instead of completing a single training course and moving on, employees can engage in ongoing, dynamic learning experiences that evolve as their skills and roles change.

AI-powered platforms can track employee performance over time, identify areas for improvement, and recommend new learning opportunities that align with their career goals. This continuous feedback loop allows employees to upskill and reskill more effectively, keeping pace with the rapidly changing demands of the workplace.

For example, an AI system might detect that an employee has mastered a particular skill and recommend new training to help them develop leadership abilities. Alternatively, the system could identify emerging industry trends and suggest relevant courses to keep the employee ahead of the curve.

By fostering a culture of continuous learning, AI and machine learning help organizations build a more adaptable, resilient workforce.

Real-World Examples of AI and Machine Learning in Training

1. IBM's Watson AI in Corporate Training

IBM's Watson AI is a prime example of how AI is transforming corporate training. Watson uses natural language processing and machine learning to analyze data from employees' interactions with training materials, personalizing the learning experience in real time. Watson can recommend specific training modules, assess employee performance, and even predict future learning needs based on individual and organizational goals.

By using Watson's AI-powered platform, companies can ensure that employees receive the right training at the right time, improving learning outcomes and overall business performance.

2. Microsoft's AI-Powered Learning Tools

Microsoft has integrated AI into its suite of learning tools, using machine learning algorithms to personalize training experiences for employees. Microsoft's AI-driven platforms provide tailored content recommendations, real-time assessments, and continuous feedback, making it easier for employees to learn new skills and improve their performance.

Microsoft's AI tools also leverage data to identify skills gaps across the organization, helping HR teams design more effective training programs and allocate resources where they are needed most.

3. **Google's AI for Skills Development**

Google uses AI and machine learning to power its internal training programs, offering employees personalized learning paths based on their roles, skills, and career aspirations. Google's AI systems can identify the skills that employees need to develop, recommend relevant courses, and track progress over time.

This approach has allowed Google to create a continuous learning environment that keeps employees engaged, motivated, and ready to take on new challenges.

Another compelling example of how AI is revolutionizing corporate training can be seen in Amazon's implementation of an AI-driven learning platform.

Case Study: Amazon's AI Ready Initiative for Workforce Training[1]

Overview:
Amazon recognized the growing demand for AI skills in the workplace, as companies increasingly adopt AI technologies. In response, Amazon launched the AI Ready initiative, aiming to provide free AI training to 2 million people globally by 2025. The initiative addresses the significant gap between the need for AI talent and the availability of skilled workers, while highlighting the potential for employees with AI skills to earn up to 47% more in salaries.

Solution:
To achieve this goal, Amazon introduced several new initiatives, including eight free AI and generative AI courses, scholarships for high school and university students, and a collaboration with Code.org to teach students about AI through interactive projects. These programs are designed to make AI education accessible to both technical and non-technical audiences, offering a range of courses from foundational AI concepts to advanced technical skills like machine learning and AI application development.

Results:
Amazon's AI Ready initiative is expected to bridge the AI talent gap and create opportunities for workers to upskill in AI. With more than 50,000

scholarships provided and a variety of free resources available, the program enables individuals to increase their earning potential and prepares businesses for a future where AI will play a pivotal role in operations. The initiative also promotes the inclusion of underrepresented communities in AI education, ensuring a more diverse AI workforce.

The Future of AI and Machine Learning in Training

As AI and machine learning technologies continue to advance, the potential for transforming corporate training will only grow. In the future, we can expect AI-driven platforms to become even more sophisticated, offering hyper-personalized learning experiences that are fully integrated with employees' daily workflows.

Emerging trends such as **AI-driven mentorship programs**, **virtual reality (VR) simulations**, and **natural language processing** (NLP)-based learning assistants will create even more opportunities for employees to engage in immersive, interactive learning experiences. These technologies will enable organizations to develop more agile, adaptable, and highly skilled workforces.

Moreover, as AI becomes more adept at predicting future skills needs based on industry trends, companies will be able to proactively prepare their employees for upcoming changes, ensuring that they remain competitive in the marketplace.

Conclusion: Embracing AI and Machine Learning for the Future of Learning

AI and machine learning are not just tools for automating tasks—they are revolutionizing how organizations approach employee development. By offering personalized, data-driven learning experiences, these technologies are helping companies create more effective and efficient training programs. As AI continues to evolve, it will play an even more integral role in shaping the future of learning, offering unprecedented opportunities for organizations to build a workforce that is always ready to meet the challenges of tomorrow.

In the next chapter, we'll explore how microlearning and just-in-time learning are enhancing the adaptive and AI-driven learning systems we've discussed, providing employees with flexible, on-demand learning opportunities that fit into the flow of work.

Endnotes

1. Amazon. (2023). *Amazon aims to provide free AI skills training to 2 million people by 2025 with its new 'AI Ready' commitment.* "New Amazon AI initiative includes scholarships, free AI courses" (aboutamazon.com)

5 MICROLEARNING AND JUST-IN-TIME LEARNING

As the pace of work accelerates and employees face increasing demands on their time, traditional training methods are often seen as time-consuming and disconnected from the immediate needs of the job. In response, two modern approaches—**microlearning** and **just-in-time learning**—are emerging as essential components of workplace learning strategies. These methods focus on delivering targeted, bite-sized learning experiences that fit seamlessly into the flow of work, providing employees with the knowledge they need precisely when they need it.

In this chapter, we'll explore the concepts of microlearning and just-in-time learning, how they complement other modern learning methods, and why they are effective tools for fostering continuous development in the workplace.

What is Microlearning?

Microlearning is an approach to training that breaks down complex concepts into small, easily digestible units, typically delivered in short bursts of time. Each module, or "micro-lesson," usually lasts between 2 to 10 minutes and focuses on a single, specific topic. Microlearning can take many forms, including videos, quizzes, articles, podcasts, or interactive simulations, and it can be accessed on-demand through digital platforms.

The primary goal of microlearning is to reduce cognitive overload by presenting information in manageable chunks, allowing employees to absorb and retain knowledge more effectively. By focusing on one concept at a time, microlearning makes it easier for learners to stay engaged and apply what they've learned to their day-to-day tasks.

Why Microlearning Works

1. **Cognitive Load Reduction**

One of the key benefits of microlearning is its ability to reduce **cognitive load**—the mental effort required to process and retain information. When employees are bombarded with large amounts of information in traditional training sessions, they often struggle to retain everything they've learned. By delivering content in smaller, more manageable pieces, microlearning allows learners to focus on one topic at a time, making it easier to understand and remember.

2. **Increased Engagement**

Employees are more likely to engage with training content when it's short, relevant, and immediately applicable. Microlearning's bite-sized approach allows learners to fit training into their schedules without feeling overwhelmed. Whether they're on a coffee break, commuting, or have a few spare minutes between tasks, employees can easily access microlearning modules whenever it's convenient for them.

This flexibility encourages more frequent interaction with learning content, leading to better retention and higher completion rates compared to traditional, lengthy training sessions.

3. **Just-in-Time Learning Reinforcement**

Microlearning is especially powerful when combined with **just-in-time learning**—the delivery of training content at the exact moment an employee needs it to perform a task. For example, an employee about to conduct a performance review can quickly review a short microlearning module on giving feedback. This ensures that the knowledge is fresh and immediately applicable, reinforcing the learning experience and helping employees perform their tasks more effectively.

4. **Mobile Accessibility**

In an increasingly mobile workforce, microlearning's digital-first nature makes it highly accessible. Employees can engage with microlearning content on their phones, tablets, or laptops, making it easy to learn on the go. This accessibility is especially important for remote workers, field workers, or employees in industries where time away from the job is limited.

5. **Supports Continuous Learning**

Microlearning encourages a **culture of continuous learning**. Because it's quick and accessible, employees can engage with learning content regularly, rather than viewing training as a one-time event. Over time, this leads to the incremental buildup of knowledge, reinforcing key concepts and promoting long-term retention.

Examples of Microlearning in Action

- **Retail**: A sales associate might complete a 5-minute microlearning module on the latest product features before starting a shift, ensuring they're prepared to answer customer questions with up-to-date information.

- **Healthcare**: Nurses and medical staff can access short tutorials on new procedures or protocols before treating a patient, allowing them to review important information without disrupting patient care.

- **Customer Service**: A customer service representative can review a quick lesson on handling difficult clients just before starting a call, helping them to apply the right techniques in real time.

A great example of microlearning in action is Walmart's approach to training its frontline workers. Here's how they effectively used microlearning to address training challenges at scale:

Case Study: Walmart's Use of Microlearning and Gamification for Safety[1]

Overview:
Walmart aimed to improve its safety culture and reduce workplace accidents. Given the size of the organization, even a small reduction in safety incidents would yield significant cost savings. Walmart recognized the need for an engaging and effective training approach to boost employees' safety knowledge and practices.

Solution:
Walmart implemented a microlearning and gamification program to support employee learning. The program delivered short, interactive lessons on safety practices, making it easier for employees to engage and retain the information. By incorporating gamification elements, Walmart encouraged voluntary participation and created a more engaging training experience.

Results:
Walmart's safety program achieved impressive results, with a 91% voluntary participation rate and a 54% reduction in recorded safety incidents. These improvements not only enhanced workplace safety but also translated into significant financial savings for the company.

What is Just-in-Time Learning?

While microlearning focuses on delivering content in small units, **just-in-time learning** ensures that this content is available at the moment it's needed. This approach empowers employees by providing them with immediate, on-demand access to the information and skills they need to perform a task effectively.

Just-in-time learning is the perfect solution for today's fast-paced work environments, where employees often encounter new challenges or tasks that require quick reference to a specific piece of knowledge. Whether it's reviewing a safety procedure, learning how to operate a new piece of equipment, or preparing for a client meeting, just-in-time learning ensures that employees have the resources they need to succeed, exactly when they need them.

The Benefits of Just-in-Time Learning

1. **Immediate Application**

The primary advantage of just-in-time learning is that it allows employees to apply new knowledge or skills immediately. This creates a direct link between learning and performance, making the training more relevant and impactful. Rather than waiting for a scheduled training session or trying to remember information learned weeks or months earlier, employees can access the material in real time, when it's most useful.

2. **Increased Efficiency**

Just-in-time learning is efficient because it eliminates the need for employees to sit through lengthy, generalized training sessions that may not be immediately relevant to their work. Instead, employees can quickly find the specific information they need and get back to their tasks, minimizing downtime and maximizing productivity.

3. **Supports Performance Support Systems**

Just-in-time learning is often integrated into **performance support systems**—tools that provide employees with instant access to job aids, tutorials, and other resources they need to complete tasks. For example, a software engineer might use an integrated help feature within their development environment to quickly learn how to use a new tool, rather than searching for external resources or waiting for formal training.

4. **Minimizes Forgetting**

One of the major challenges of traditional learning approaches is the **forgetting curve**—the tendency to forget newly acquired information over time. Just-in-time learning minimizes this issue by delivering knowledge at the point of need, ensuring that employees use the information immediately and reinforce their learning through application.

5. **Flexible and Responsive**

Just-in-time learning can respond to the rapidly changing needs of the workplace. When new processes, tools, or regulations are introduced, organizations can quickly provide employees with the necessary training in a just-in-time format. This ensures that employees are always up-to-date with the latest information and skills, without the need for lengthy retraining sessions.

Examples of Just-in-Time Learning in Action

- **Manufacturing**: A factory worker can scan a QR code on a machine to watch a short video tutorial on performing maintenance, providing immediate guidance without needing to leave the workstation.

- **Finance**: A financial advisor preparing for a client meeting can pull up a quick guide on new investment strategies, allowing them to enter the meeting with the most up-to-date knowledge.

- **Sales**: A sales team can access a checklist or microlearning module about a new product feature moments before a sales call, ensuring they have the latest information ready to share with the client.

How Microlearning and Just-in-Time Learning Work Together

Microlearning and just-in-time learning are complementary strategies that, when combined, provide a powerful learning experience. Microlearning provides the content in small, digestible units, while just-in-time learning ensures that this content is available precisely when it's needed. Together, they make learning more efficient, engaging, and effective.

For example, an employee in the hospitality industry might access a microlearning module on customer service while on their lunch break. Later, during their shift, they encounter a difficult customer and use just-in-time learning to quickly review conflict resolution strategies. This combination allows the employee to learn both proactively and reactively, reinforcing their skills and applying them in real-world situations.

Implementing Microlearning and Just-in-Time Learning in Your Organization

1. **Identify Critical Moments of Need**

The first step in implementing just-in-time learning is identifying the moments when employees are most likely to need immediate access to information. These are often moments of transition—such as when employees are taking on a new role, using new tools, or dealing with an unfamiliar situation. By pinpointing these moments, organizations can ensure that the right content is available at the right time.

2. Leverage Technology

Technology is essential for delivering microlearning and just-in-time learning at scale. Learning management systems (LMS), mobile learning platforms, and performance support systems are all key tools for making content easily accessible. For just-in-time learning, consider integrating learning resources directly into the tools and platforms employees already use, such as embedding tutorials within software or using QR codes on physical equipment.

3. Create a Library of Bite-Sized Content

To support both microlearning and just-in-time learning, organizations need to build a library of short, targeted learning resources that employees can access quickly. These resources should be searchable, modular, and categorized based on key competencies, tasks, or roles. Additionally, it's important to regularly update this library to ensure that content remains relevant and aligned with changing business needs.

4. Promote a Learning Culture

To successfully implement microlearning and just-in-time learning, organizations must promote a culture that values continuous learning. This means encouraging employees to take advantage of learning opportunities whenever they arise and rewarding proactive engagement with learning resources. By fostering a growth mindset, organizations can ensure that employees are motivated to continuously develop their skills and knowledge.

Conclusion: The Power of Bite-Sized, On-Demand Learning

Microlearning and just-in-time learning represent a shift away from traditional, structured training programs toward a more flexible, responsive approach. These methods recognize that learning doesn't have to be confined to formal sessions—it can happen in short bursts, on-demand, and in the moment of need. By embracing these strategies, organizations can ensure that employees are equipped with the knowledge and skills they need to thrive in a fast-paced, ever-changing work environment.

Endnotes

1. HR Exchange. (2018). *How Walmart used gamification to address safety practices.* How Walmart used gamification to address safety practices (hrexchangenetwork.com)

6 PERSONALIZED LEARNING JOURNEYS FOR EVERY EMPLOYEE

In today's diverse and dynamic workforce, a one-size-fits-all approach to training and development is no longer effective. Employees come to work with varying levels of experience, skills, and career goals, and each individual's learning style and needs are different. Recognizing these differences, forward-thinking organizations are shifting toward creating **personalized learning journeys** that cater to each employee's unique path.

A personalized learning journey is more than just a training program; it's a continuous, evolving experience that aligns an employee's learning and development with their individual aspirations, job role, and the company's goals. By designing learning journeys that are tailored to the needs of each employee, organizations can not only improve engagement and retention but also foster a culture of growth and development that benefits the entire organization.

In this chapter, we'll explore the concept of personalized learning journeys, how they work, and the steps organizations can take to implement them successfully.

What Is a Personalized Learning Journey?

A **personalized learning journey** is a customized path that guides an employee through the process of acquiring new skills, knowledge, and experiences based on their individual needs, job requirements, and career ambitions. Rather than following a rigid, standardized training program, employees on a personalized learning journey engage in a mix of learning experiences that are tailored to their specific context.

This journey is often dynamic, evolving over time as the employee develops and as new business needs emerge. It can include a wide range of learning activities, from formal courses and certifications to on-the-job training, mentoring, microlearning, and just-in-time learning.

Why Personalization Matters

1. **Different Roles Require Different Skills**

In a diverse organization, employees in different roles often need very different skills to be successful. For example, a software engineer will require deep technical training in coding languages and problem-solving techniques, while a marketing professional might need more creative training on storytelling, data analysis, or brand strategy. A standardized learning program may not be relevant for all employees, and without personalization, organizations risk wasting time and resources on training that doesn't meet individual needs.

2. **Individual Learning Styles**

Not all employees learn the same way. Some people prefer visual content, while others may absorb information better through hands-on experiences, reading, or listening. A personalized learning journey takes these preferences into account, allowing employees to engage with content in the format that works best for them. By respecting these individual learning styles, organizations can ensure better retention and application of knowledge.

3. **Career Goals and Aspirations**

Employees have different career goals and ambitions. Some may want to climb the corporate ladder, while others may seek lateral moves into new departments or roles. Personalized learning journeys take these aspirations into account, aligning training and development with each individual's long-term career objectives. This alignment fosters a sense of purpose and motivation, as employees see how their learning connects directly to their personal and professional growth.

Key Elements of a Personalized Learning Journey

Creating a personalized learning journey involves more than just offering a variety of training courses. It requires a holistic approach that incorporates multiple elements, including continuous assessment, adaptable content, and support from managers and mentors. Below are the key elements that make personalized learning journeys successful.

1. **Continuous Assessment and Feedback**

At the heart of a personalized learning journey is the ability to assess an employee's skills, performance, and progress continuously. This can be achieved through self-assessments, manager feedback, peer reviews, or even AI-driven learning platforms that track performance in real time. Continuous assessment allows the learning path to be adjusted dynamically, ensuring that the employee is always working on the right areas for growth and improvement.

For example, an employee may start their journey by learning basic project management skills, but after completing several projects successfully, their learning path might shift toward more advanced leadership or strategic management training.

2. **Tailored Learning Content**

The content of a personalized learning journey should be flexible and adaptable to the learner's needs. AI and adaptive learning platforms play a key role in this, offering curated learning materials based on an employee's progress, interests, and knowledge gaps. Employees might start with foundational courses and then move on to more specialized content as they master the basics.

Tailored learning content can take many forms, including:

- **Formal courses** (online or in-person)
- **Microlearning modules** on specific topics
- **Interactive simulations** or real-world case studies
- **On-the-job training** for practical skills application
- **Peer learning** and knowledge-sharing sessions

By offering a variety of learning options, organizations give employees the flexibility to engage with the material that resonates most with their needs.

3. **Career Pathways and Development Plans**

A personalized learning journey should be closely tied to an employee's career development plan. By aligning learning with career pathways, employees can see a clear connection between their current role and their future aspirations. This creates a sense of purpose and motivation, as employees understand that the skills they are developing today will help them reach their long-term goals.

For example, an entry-level employee may follow a learning journey that builds basic competencies in their current role but also includes training that prepares them for a future leadership position. As they progress, their learning journey evolves, introducing more complex, strategic content that aligns with their new responsibilities.

4. **Mentorship and Coaching**

A successful personalized learning journey often involves mentorship and coaching. While formal learning programs are important, the guidance and feedback from more experienced colleagues can significantly enhance an employee's development. Mentors can offer insights based on real-world experience, provide career advice, and help employees navigate challenges as they progress along their learning path.

Coaching from managers is equally important. Managers can help employees identify learning opportunities, set goals, and provide feedback on their progress. This active involvement ensures that the learning journey is aligned with both the employee's goals and the organization's strategic objectives.

5. **Integration of Technology**

Technology is a critical enabler of personalized learning journeys. AI-powered learning platforms, learning management systems (LMS), and mobile learning tools allow organizations to deliver customized content, track progress, and provide real-time feedback. These systems also give employees the flexibility to learn at their own pace, accessing materials whenever and wherever it's most convenient for them.

For example, a sales representative might use a mobile learning platform to complete product training on the go, while an HR professional might access leadership development modules through a desktop LMS. Technology ensures that learning is always accessible, regardless of an employee's location or schedule.

The Benefits of Personalized Learning Journeys

1. **Improved Engagement and Motivation**

Employees are more engaged and motivated when they feel that their learning experiences are relevant to their needs and goals. Personalized learning journeys create a sense of ownership over development, making employees more invested in the learning process. This engagement leads to better retention of information and greater enthusiasm for ongoing growth.

2. **Enhanced Skill Development**

Because personalized learning journeys are tailored to each individual, they focus on the specific skills that are most relevant to the employee's current role and future aspirations. This targeted approach ensures that employees are developing the right skills at the right time, leading to more effective performance and quicker skill acquisition.

3. **Better Retention and Career Growth**

Employees who feel supported in their development are more likely to stay with an organization. Personalized learning journeys demonstrate that the company values their growth and is invested in their long-term success. This not only improves retention but also helps organizations build a pipeline of skilled, capable leaders who are ready to take on new challenges as the business evolves.

4. **Alignment with Business Goals**

When learning journeys are personalized, they can be closely aligned with both the employee's career goals and the organization's strategic objectives. This alignment ensures that the development of skills and knowledge supports the company's needs, helping to drive business success. For example, an organization focused on digital transformation might tailor learning journeys to include training on AI, data analytics, or digital marketing, ensuring that employees are prepared to contribute to key initiatives.

Creating Personalized Learning Journeys in Your Organization

To successfully implement personalized learning journeys, organizations must take a strategic and holistic approach. Here are the steps to get started:

1. **Assess Individual Needs and Goals**

Start by understanding the unique needs, skills, and career aspirations of each employee. This can be done through self-assessments, manager reviews, and feedback sessions. Identifying these individual needs will allow you to tailor learning journeys that align with each employee's current role and future ambitions.

2. **Leverage Technology**

Use AI-powered learning platforms and LMS systems to deliver personalized content at scale. These platforms allow you to track progress, provide real-time feedback, and curate learning materials that are relevant to each employee's goals.

3. **Align with Career Development Plans**

Work with employees and managers to create career development plans that outline long-term goals and identify the skills needed to achieve them. Use these plans as a roadmap for building personalized learning journeys that evolve over time.

4. **Provide Ongoing Support**

Offer employees continuous support through mentorship, coaching, and regular feedback. Ensure that managers are actively involved in the learning process, helping employees stay on track and making adjustments to the learning journey as needed.

5. **Measure Success**

Track the effectiveness of personalized learning journeys by measuring key performance indicators (KPIs) such as employee engagement, skill acquisition, and career progression. Use this data to refine and improve the learning journey for future employees.

Conclusion: Tailoring Learning for Long-Term Success

Personalized learning journeys represent a powerful shift in how organizations approach employee development. By recognizing the unique needs, skills, and aspirations of each individual, organizations can create learning experiences that are more engaging, effective, and aligned with both personal and organizational goals. As businesses continue to evolve, the ability to offer personalized, dynamic learning journeys will be key to building a skilled, motivated workforce that is ready to tackle the challenges of the future.

In the next chapter, we'll explore how to build a culture of continuous learning within your organization and how personalized learning journeys contribute to creating an agile, growth-oriented workforce.

7 BUILDING A CULTURE OF CONTINUOUS LEARNING

In an era defined by rapid technological advancements, shifting industry landscapes, and constant innovation, organizations can no longer afford to rely solely on one-off training programs or static skill sets. To stay competitive, businesses must foster a **culture of continuous learning**, where employees are encouraged to develop new skills, challenge their current understanding, and adapt to evolving demands. This chapter explores what it means to create a learning culture and provides actionable steps for embedding continuous learning into the fabric of your organization.

What is a Culture of Continuous Learning?

A **culture of continuous learning** is an organizational environment that prioritizes learning and development as an ongoing process. In such a culture, learning isn't limited to formal training sessions or workshops; instead, it becomes an integral part of daily operations and is driven by curiosity, collaboration, and the desire to grow both personally and professionally.

Continuous learning cultures recognize that:

- Learning is never "finished"—it is a lifelong process.
- Employees at all levels, from front-line staff to executives, must actively engage in learning.
- The organization supports and provides the tools and resources necessary for growth.

Why is Continuous Learning Critical?

1. **Keeping Pace with Change**

Industries are evolving faster than ever, with new technologies, processes, and regulations emerging at a rapid pace. Organizations that fail to adapt risk being left behind. A culture of continuous learning equips employees with the mindset and skills needed to keep pace with these changes, ensuring that the company remains agile and competitive.

2. **Fostering Innovation**

Innovation thrives in environments where learning is encouraged. When employees are given the freedom to explore new ideas, test theories, and acquire knowledge, they are more likely to develop innovative solutions that drive business success. Continuous learning promotes a mindset of experimentation and creativity, both of which are essential for innovation.

3. **Employee Engagement and Retention**

Employees are more engaged when they feel that their organization is invested in their personal and professional growth. A culture of continuous learning gives employees the tools and opportunities to advance their careers, which increases job satisfaction and loyalty. In turn, organizations benefit from higher retention rates and a more motivated workforce.

4. **Preparing for Future Skills Needs**

As automation, artificial intelligence, and digital transformation reshape industries, the skills employees need to succeed are constantly changing. A culture of continuous learning helps organizations stay ahead of these shifts by proactively upskilling and reskilling their workforce. Employees are better prepared for future roles, and the organization can more easily fill skills gaps without relying solely on external hires.

Key Elements of a Continuous Learning Culture

Building a culture of continuous learning requires intentional effort and support at every level of the organization. Below are the key elements that contribute to fostering such a culture.

1. **Leadership Buy-In and Role Modeling**

Leadership commitment is essential for creating a continuous learning culture. Leaders must not only support learning initiatives but also model learning behaviours themselves. When employees see that their leaders are engaged in their own development—whether by attending training sessions, seeking feedback, or pursuing certifications—it sends a powerful message that learning is a priority.

Leaders can encourage continuous learning by:

- Setting the example by engaging in professional development.
- Communicating the importance of learning in achieving organizational goals.
- Allocating resources (time, budget, technology) to support learning efforts.
- Celebrating learning milestones and achievements publicly.

2. **Learning as a Core Value**

Organizations with a culture of continuous learning embed learning and development into their core values. This means that learning isn't seen as an extra task or a once-a-year requirement—it's a fundamental part of how the business operates. Employees should understand that learning is not just encouraged but expected, and that it directly ties into their performance and career advancement.

Ways to integrate learning into organizational values include:

- Including learning and development goals in performance reviews.
- Linking learning initiatives to the company's strategic objectives.
- Creating formal and informal opportunities for employees to share their learning experiences.

3. **Access to Learning Opportunities and Resources**

A continuous learning culture requires that employees have easy access to a variety of learning opportunities and resources. This includes formal training programs, but also informal learning experiences such as peer mentoring, collaborative projects, and on-the-job learning.

Key resources and tools for continuous learning include:

- **Learning Management Systems (LMS)**: Provide employees with a central hub for accessing training courses, certifications, and learning content.
- **Mobile Learning Platforms**: Allow employees to learn anytime, anywhere, providing flexibility and convenience.
- **Learning Communities**: Foster collaboration and knowledge-sharing through forums, discussion groups, and peer-to-peer learning.
- **Coaching and Mentorship Programs**: Pair employees with mentors who can offer guidance, support, and feedback on their development.

4. **Encouraging Curiosity and Exploration**

A continuous learning culture encourages curiosity and exploration. Employees should feel empowered to ask questions, seek new knowledge, and challenge the status quo. When curiosity is embraced, employees are more likely to engage in self-directed learning, explore new areas of interest, and develop a growth mindset.

Organizations can cultivate curiosity by:

- Creating safe spaces for asking questions and proposing new ideas.
- Offering employees the time and freedom to pursue learning opportunities that align with their interests.
- Recognizing and rewarding employees who take initiative in their learning.

5. **Promoting Feedback and Reflection**

Feedback and reflection are critical components of continuous learning. Employees need regular, constructive feedback to understand their strengths, identify areas for improvement, and refine their skills. Additionally, creating opportunities for reflection helps employees internalize their learning experiences and apply them more effectively.

Encourage feedback and reflection by:

- Implementing 360-degree feedback systems that allow employees to receive input from peers, managers, and subordinates.
- Incorporating reflection activities into training programs, such as journaling or peer discussions.
- Encouraging self-assessment and goal-setting based on past learning experiences.

6. **Fostering a Growth Mindset**

A **growth mindset**, a term popularized by psychologist Carol Dweck, is the belief that skills and abilities can be developed through effort, learning, and persistence. In a culture of continuous learning, a growth mindset is essential. Employees with a growth mindset view challenges as opportunities for learning rather than threats, and they are more willing to take risks, make mistakes, and learn from them.

To foster a growth mindset within the organization:

- Emphasize the importance of effort and learning, rather than focusing solely on outcomes.
- Encourage experimentation and learning from failure.

- Offer employees opportunities to step outside their comfort zones and tackle new challenges.

- Reinforce the idea that mistakes are part of the learning process.

One example of an organization that has successfully embedded a culture of continuous learning through the promotion of a growth mindset is Microsoft. Here's how they transformed their culture:

Case Study: Microsoft's Growth Mindset and Continuous Learning[1]

Overview:
Microsoft underwent a cultural transformation under CEO Satya Nadella, emphasizing the importance of continuous learning and a growth mindset for all employees, from frontline workers to executives.

Solution:
Microsoft focused on fostering a **growth mindset** by encouraging employees to take ownership of their learning and development. The company revamped its learning infrastructure, offering a wide range of courses, certifications, and learning tools through LinkedIn Learning and other platforms. They also embedded learning into everyday work processes, making it a part of the company culture.

Results:
This shift led to a more innovative and agile workforce. Employees embraced continuous learning, which contributed to Microsoft's resurgence in innovation and the successful launch of new products. The company's employee engagement and satisfaction scores also increased significantly.

The Role of Technology in Supporting Continuous Learning

Technology plays a key role in enabling continuous learning at scale. With the right tools and platforms, organizations can provide employees with on-demand access to learning resources, track progress, and offer personalized learning experiences that meet the unique needs of each individual.

Key technologies that support continuous learning include:

1. **Learning Management Systems (LMS)**: LMS platforms centralize learning resources and allow employees to engage with training materials at their own pace. These systems also provide analytics and reporting tools that help organizations measure the effectiveness of their learning initiatives.

2. **AI-Powered Learning Platforms**: AI-driven platforms use machine learning algorithms to personalize learning experiences, recommending content based on an employee's skills, performance, and career goals. This ensures that employees receive the most relevant learning opportunities at the right time.

3. **Microlearning and Mobile Learning**: Microlearning platforms deliver bite-sized content that employees can engage with on the go. This makes it easier for employees to fit learning into their busy schedules and reinforces a habit of continuous development.

4. **Collaborative Tools**: Platforms like Slack, Microsoft Teams, or internal wikis enable employees to collaborate, share knowledge, and learn from one another in real time. These tools foster a culture of knowledge sharing, where learning is a collective, ongoing process.

Measuring the Impact of Continuous Learning

To ensure the success of a continuous learning culture, organizations must track and measure the impact of their learning initiatives. This involves more than just counting the number of training sessions completed; it requires looking at how learning translates into improved performance, innovation, and business outcomes.

Metrics for evaluating continuous learning may include:

- **Employee Engagement**: Are employees actively participating in learning initiatives? Do they feel supported in their development?

- **Skill Acquisition and Development**: Are employees developing the skills needed to succeed in their current roles and future positions? Is the organization closing skills gaps?

- **Performance Improvement**: How has continuous learning impacted individual and team performance? Are employees able to apply their learning to achieve better outcomes?

- **Innovation and Problem-Solving**: Are employees using their learning to generate new ideas and solve complex problems?

- **Retention and Career Progression**: Are employees staying with the organization and advancing in their careers due to learning opportunities?

Building a Sustainable Learning Culture: Best Practices

1. **Start with Leadership**: Leadership sets the tone for the organization's learning culture. Ensure that leaders are committed to continuous learning and model learning behaviours for their teams.

2. **Embed Learning into Daily Work**: Make learning a natural part of the workday by integrating it into workflows, meetings, and team discussions. Encourage employees to share their learning experiences with colleagues.

3. **Provide Ongoing Support**: Offer employees the tools, resources, and time they need to engage in continuous learning. Ensure that learning is accessible, flexible, and relevant to their roles.

4. **Recognize and Reward Learning**: Celebrate learning achievements and recognize employees who are actively pursuing development. This reinforces the value of learning and encourages others to follow suit.

5. **Adapt and Evolve**: A continuous learning culture is never static. Regularly review and update learning initiatives to ensure they align with changing business needs and employee aspirations.

Conclusion: Creating a Culture of Lifelong Learning

Building a culture of continuous learning is about more than just offering training programs—it's about creating an environment where learning is a core part of the organization's identity. By fostering curiosity, supporting growth, and providing the resources employees need to succeed, organizations can build a workforce that is not only skilled and adaptable but also motivated to keep learning throughout their careers.

In the next chapter, we'll explore the specific strategies for reskilling and upskilling employees to meet the demands of a rapidly changing workforce, and how organizations can prepare their people for the future of work.

Endnotes

1. Microsoft. (2020). *How Microsoft built a learning culture.* How Microsoft built a learning culture - Microsoft Community Hub]

8 RESKILLING AND UPSKILLING FOR THE FUTURE

As industries evolve and new technologies emerge, the skills required to succeed in the workplace are shifting at an unprecedented rate. Automation, artificial intelligence, digital transformation, and the growing demand for sustainability are fundamentally reshaping the global job market. To thrive in this rapidly changing environment, organizations must focus on two critical strategies: **reskilling** and **upskilling**.

Reskilling refers to training employees in new skills to transition into different roles within the organization, while upskilling involves enhancing existing skills to help employees grow within their current roles. Both strategies are essential for maintaining a competitive, adaptable workforce in an era where traditional career paths are no longer linear, and the pace of change demands continuous development.

In this chapter, we'll explore the importance of reskilling and upskilling, how to identify the skills your workforce will need in the future, and how organizations can implement effective reskilling and upskilling programs to prepare employees for the jobs of tomorrow.

Why Reskilling and Upskilling Are Critical for the Future

1. **Technological Disruption**

Technological advancements are transforming industries at a speed that many businesses struggle to keep up with. Automation and AI are taking over repetitive and manual tasks, while the demand for digital literacy is increasing across all sectors. As a result, some jobs are disappearing, while new roles are being created that require a completely different skill set.

To remain relevant in this new landscape, employees must be reskilled for emerging roles that are driven by technology. Meanwhile, those who are already in roles affected by technology need upskilling to better leverage new tools and platforms.

2. **Bridging the Skills Gap**

According to numerous studies, there is a growing gap between the skills that employers need and the skills that the workforce currently possesses. For example, roles in data analytics, cybersecurity, and cloud computing are in high demand, but many workers lack the expertise to fill these positions. Upskilling current employees allows organizations to close this gap by developing the talent they already have, rather than relying on external hires to fill every role.

Reskilling helps prevent the obsolescence of employees whose roles are being automated or phased out. By identifying transferable skills and offering training in new areas, organizations can redeploy workers into high-demand roles rather than letting valuable talent go.

3. **Employee Retention and Engagement**

Providing opportunities for growth through reskilling and upskilling is not only a strategic response to external market forces but also a key driver of employee engagement and retention. When employees see that their organization is invested in their professional development and committed to helping them succeed in the future workforce, they are more likely to stay and contribute to the company's success.

Moreover, upskilling gives employees the chance to take on more challenging and rewarding tasks, increasing job satisfaction and reducing the likelihood of burnout.

4. **Future-Proofing the Workforce**

The concept of **future-proofing** involves preparing your workforce for roles and challenges that may not even exist yet. By fostering a culture of continuous learning and development, organizations can ensure that employees are adaptable, resilient, and equipped to handle the uncertainties of tomorrow's job market. Reskilling and upskilling are key components of this strategy, as they help employees stay ahead of industry trends and maintain relevance as the workforce evolves.

Identifying the Skills Needed for the Future

Before implementing reskilling and upskilling programs, organizations must first identify the skills that will be in demand in the coming years. This requires understanding both internal and external factors, such as technological trends, business goals, and market demands.

1. **Assessing Industry Trends**

To determine which skills will be critical for the future, organizations must stay informed about industry trends and emerging technologies. For example, roles in data science, machine learning, and digital marketing are becoming increasingly important across many sectors, while traditional roles in manufacturing or manual labour may decline as automation takes over.

In addition to technical skills, **human-centric skills** such as emotional intelligence, adaptability, creativity, and leadership will remain highly valuable, as these are areas where humans outperform machines. By focusing on both technical and soft skills, organizations can develop a well-rounded workforce capable of thriving in any environment.

2. **Conducting a Skills Audit**

A **skills audit** helps organizations identify the current skills within their workforce and highlight any gaps that need to be addressed through reskilling or upskilling. This involves assessing employees' existing capabilities, comparing them to the skills required for future roles, and identifying areas where additional training is needed.

For example, if your organization is undergoing a digital transformation, you might find that certain employees need training in cloud computing, cybersecurity, or digital project management. By conducting regular skills audits, organizations can ensure that they are proactively addressing skill gaps rather than reacting to them after they become a critical issue.

3. **Aligning Skills Development with Business Goals**

Reskilling and upskilling efforts should be aligned with the organization's long-term business objectives. For example, if your company is expanding into new markets or launching new products, you'll need to ensure that employees have the necessary skills to support these initiatives. This could involve upskilling teams in areas such as market analysis, customer engagement, or product development.

By linking skills development to business goals, organizations can create a workforce that is not only prepared for the future but also actively contributes to the company's growth and success.

Implementing Reskilling and Upskilling Programs

Once the necessary skills have been identified, the next step is to design and implement effective reskilling and upskilling programs. These programs should be flexible, accessible, and tailored to the needs of individual employees and teams.

1. **Tailored Learning Pathways**

A successful reskilling or upskilling program should offer **personalized learning pathways** that cater to the specific needs of each employee. Some employees may need to be reskilled for entirely new roles, while others may simply need to enhance their current capabilities. By tailoring learning experiences to the individual, organizations can ensure that each employee is developing the right skills at the right time.

For example, an IT professional may need to upskill in cybersecurity to stay current with new threats, while a factory worker may need to be reskilled in operating advanced robotics. Personalized learning pathways can include a mix of online courses, hands-on training, mentorship, and certification programs.

2. **Leverage Technology for Learning**

Technology plays a key role in facilitating reskilling and upskilling efforts. **AI-powered learning platforms, learning management systems (LMS)**, and **mobile learning apps** make it easier to deliver personalized content at scale, track employee progress, and provide real-time feedback. These tools also allow employees to learn at their own pace, whether in the office, at home, or on the go.

Microlearning, which delivers content in small, easily digestible chunks, is particularly effective for upskilling employees who may have limited time for formal training. By offering flexible learning options, organizations can ensure that employees have continuous access to the skills they need to succeed.

3. **Mentorship and Peer Learning**

While technology is essential, **mentorship and peer learning** remain invaluable components of reskilling and upskilling programs. Experienced employees can share their knowledge and provide guidance to those who are learning new skills. This collaborative approach not only accelerates the learning process but also fosters a sense of community and mutual support.

For example, a senior data analyst might mentor junior employees as they learn new data visualization tools, while a team leader might facilitate peer-learning sessions where employees can share best practices and solutions to common challenges.

4. **Incorporate On-the-Job Learning**

Reskilling and upskilling should not be confined to formal training sessions. **On-the-job learning** allows employees to apply new skills in real-world situations, reinforcing their knowledge and building confidence. This approach can include job rotations, stretch assignments, or working on cross-functional teams where employees can gain hands-on experience in new areas.

For example, an employee being reskilled for a project management role might be given the opportunity to manage a small project under the guidance of an experienced mentor. This practical experience complements formal learning and helps employees build the skills they need to succeed in their new roles.

5. **Create a Supportive Environment**

Creating a supportive environment is critical to the success of reskilling and upskilling programs. Employees must feel empowered to take risks, learn from mistakes, and ask for help when needed. Encouraging a growth mindset, where employees view challenges as opportunities for learning, is key to fostering this kind of environment.

Leaders and managers should actively support employees' development by providing regular feedback, recognizing achievements, and offering encouragement. A culture of continuous learning ensures that reskilling and upskilling are seen as ongoing processes rather than one-time events.

One company that has successfully implemented a large-scale reskilling initiative is AT&T. Here's how their Future Ready program helped prepare their workforce for the digital age:

Case Study: AT&T's Massive Reskilling Initiative[1]

Overview:
Facing rapid technological change, AT&T recognized that nearly half of its workforce lacked the necessary skills for future roles in the company, particularly in areas like software development and cloud computing.

Solution:
AT&T launched a $1 billion reskilling initiative called **Future Ready** to reskill and upskill its employees. The program offered employees opportunities to take online courses, attend boot camps, and earn new certifications in areas like data science, software engineering, and cybersecurity. AT&T partnered with Coursera, Udacity, and Georgia Tech to offer a range of learning opportunities, including formal degrees.

Results:
AT&T's reskilling efforts were highly successful, with many employees transitioning into new roles within the company. This initiative not only helped AT&T retain valuable talent but also positioned the company for success in the digital age by building a future-ready workforce.

Measuring the Success of Reskilling and Upskilling Programs

To evaluate the effectiveness of reskilling and upskilling initiatives, organizations must establish clear metrics and track progress over time. Some key metrics include:

1. **Skill Acquisition and Proficiency**

Measure the specific skills employees have gained through reskilling or upskilling programs. This can be assessed through tests, practical demonstrations, certifications, or performance reviews. Tracking skill acquisition ensures that employees are mastering the competencies required for future roles.

2. **Employee Performance and Productivity**

Evaluate how reskilled or upskilled employees are performing in their new roles. Are they more productive? Are they delivering higher-quality work? Increased performance is a strong indicator that employees are successfully applying their new skills to their jobs.

3. **Internal Mobility**

Track the number of employees who transition into new roles or take on additional responsibilities after completing reskilling or upskilling programs. Internal mobility is a sign that the organization is effectively using its talent and reducing the need for external hires.

4. **Employee Retention**

Monitor retention rates among employees who have participated in reskilling or upskilling initiatives. Employees who feel supported in their development are more likely to stay with the organization, reducing turnover and fostering long-term loyalty.

Conclusion: Preparing for the Workforce of Tomorrow

Reskilling and upskilling are no longer optional—they are essential strategies for building a future-ready workforce. As industries continue to evolve, the ability to develop and redeploy talent will become a key differentiator for successful organizations. By investing in the continuous growth and development of employees, organizations can ensure that they are prepared to meet the challenges of tomorrow and remain competitive in a rapidly changing world.

Endnotes

1. Ignite. (2024). *Reskilling and Upskilling: Preparing Your Workforce for the Future of Work.* Reskilling and Upskilling: Preparing Your Workforce for the Future of Work (ignitehcm.com)

9 LEARNING BEYOND BORDERS: GLOBAL TRENDS AND REMOTE WORK

The rise of globalization and the shift to remote work have fundamentally transformed the way organizations operate, collaborate, and learn. In today's interconnected world, learning is no longer confined to physical locations or single countries—it spans borders, time zones, and cultures. As a result, workplace learning is evolving to meet the needs of a global, dispersed workforce that increasingly works remotely.

This chapter explores how global trends in learning and the growing adoption of remote work are shaping the future of employee development. We'll look at the challenges and opportunities that come with learning in a global context, how organizations can foster inclusive learning experiences across diverse regions, and the tools and strategies that are driving global learning in a remote-first world.

The Rise of Global Learning

1. **Globalization and the Need for Cross-Cultural Competence**

As businesses expand into new markets and establish operations in different countries, employees must learn to navigate a complex global landscape. Cross-cultural competence—the ability to understand and work effectively across different cultures—is no longer a nice-to-have skill; it's a necessity. Organizations need to ensure that their employees can communicate, collaborate, and adapt to the cultural norms and expectations of diverse regions.

Global learning initiatives are essential for developing this competence. By providing training in areas such as cultural sensitivity, global communication, and international business practices, organizations can equip employees with the skills they need to thrive in a globalized environment.

In addition to formal training, **peer learning and knowledge-sharing** between employees in different regions can play a vital role in building cross-cultural understanding. For example, employees in North America might share best practices with colleagues in Asia, while employees in Europe exchange insights with teams in Africa. This cross-regional collaboration fosters a culture of global learning and mutual support.

2. **The Expansion of Global Talent Pools**

Remote work has expanded the talent pool for organizations, allowing them to hire skilled employees from anywhere in the world. This shift means that learning and development programs must be flexible and adaptable to accommodate a geographically dispersed workforce with different languages, time zones, and cultural backgrounds.

To succeed in this new landscape, organizations need to create learning experiences that are **culturally inclusive** and accessible to all employees, regardless of location. This involves offering training in multiple languages, accounting for different learning preferences, and addressing the unique challenges that employees in different regions may face.

For example, an organization with employees in Latin America, Europe, and Southeast Asia might offer learning content in Spanish, English, and Mandarin, while also tailoring the material to reflect the specific challenges of each region's local market.

Remote Work: A New Era of Learning

The COVID-19 pandemic accelerated the adoption of remote work, and while many companies have since returned to in-person or hybrid models, remote work is here to stay. This shift has had profound implications for workplace learning, as organizations now need to deliver training that is not only effective but also accessible in a remote-first world.

1. **The Shift to Virtual Learning**

In a remote work environment, traditional in-person training is often no longer feasible. Instead, organizations have embraced virtual learning as a key tool for employee development. Virtual learning platforms allow employees to access training materials from anywhere, at any time, and offer the flexibility needed for a dispersed workforce.

There are several formats for virtual learning that have become essential in remote work environments:

1. **Live Webinars and Virtual Classrooms**: These offer real-time interaction between instructors and participants, simulating the experience of in-person training.
2. **Self-Paced eLearning**: Employees can access training modules on-demand, completing them at their own pace, which is particularly important for workers in different time zones.

3. **Interactive Simulations and Gamification**: These tools engage remote employees in practical learning experiences that mimic real-world scenarios, helping them apply new skills in a hands-on way.

2. **Building Connection and Collaboration in Remote Learning**

One of the challenges of remote work is the potential for isolation and disengagement. This challenge extends to remote learning, where employees may feel disconnected from their peers and the learning process itself. To counter this, organizations are increasingly using **social learning** and **collaborative tools** to foster connection and engagement.

Social learning platforms, which allow employees to share knowledge, ask questions, and collaborate on learning projects, are becoming a critical component of remote learning. By encouraging employees to interact with one another in virtual spaces, organizations can create a sense of community and support that mimics the collaborative environment of in-person training.

For example, a virtual learning community might include discussion boards, peer feedback systems, or team-based learning activities that require employees to work together to solve problems or complete assignments. These interactive elements help maintain engagement and ensure that learning is a shared experience, even when employees are physically apart.

3. **Overcoming Time Zone and Communication Barriers**

One of the biggest challenges in global remote work is coordinating across time zones and overcoming communication barriers. Learning programs need to be designed with flexibility in mind, allowing employees in different regions to participate without the constraints of traditional training schedules.

Self-paced learning modules, available through online platforms, allow employees to access content at a time that suits their local schedule. Asynchronous learning also supports flexibility, enabling employees to engage with training materials and complete assignments at their own pace, without the need to attend live sessions.

In addition, organizations must ensure that learning content is **culturally relevant** and accessible across languages. Providing multilingual training materials, incorporating diverse case studies, and respecting regional differences in communication styles are all essential to creating an inclusive learning environment that resonates with employees across the globe.

Leveraging Technology to Support Global and Remote Learning

Technology is the backbone of modern global and remote learning programs. From learning management systems (LMS) to mobile learning platforms, organizations now have a wide range of tools at their disposal to deliver effective training to employees regardless of where they are located.

1. **Learning Management Systems (LMS) for Global Reach**

A robust LMS is essential for managing learning programs that span multiple regions and time zones. These systems allow organizations to deliver and track training content on a global scale, while also providing insights into employee progress and performance. By using an LMS with built-in language support, organizations can ensure that all employees have access to training in their native language.

In addition, LMS platforms offer the flexibility to create personalized learning paths, allowing employees to engage with content that is tailored to their role, location, and individual development needs.

2. **Mobile Learning for On-the-Go Access**

In a global and remote work environment, employees may not always have access to traditional desktop computers during training. Mobile learning platforms solve this problem by allowing employees to access learning materials on their smartphones or tablets, whether they're at home, traveling, or working in the field.

Mobile learning supports both **microlearning** and **just-in-time learning**, making it easy for employees to complete short lessons or access critical information on the go. This flexibility is particularly valuable for employees in different time zones, as they can engage with training at a time that fits their schedule.

3. **AI-Driven Learning Platforms for Personalization**

Artificial intelligence (AI) is playing an increasingly important role in global learning. AI-driven platforms can analyze employee performance data, identify skills gaps, and recommend personalized learning paths based on individual needs and preferences. This level of customization is especially useful in a global context, where employees may have diverse learning backgrounds and requirements.

For example, an AI-powered learning platform might recommend different learning content for employees in the U.S. and Japan based on regional market trends, job functions, or even local industry regulations.

A great example of a company successfully implementing a global learning strategy is Siemens. Here's how they used technology to deliver consistent, accessible training across a dispersed workforce:

Case Study: Siemens' Global Learning Strategy[1]

Overview:
Siemens, a global technology company, faced the challenge of delivering consistent training across its diverse and geographically dispersed workforce. With employees spread across multiple countries and time zones, the company needed a flexible, scalable solution.

Solution:
Siemens adopted a global learning strategy through its **Learning Campus**, which provides online and mobile learning platforms accessible to employees worldwide. The company implemented self-paced learning modules available in multiple languages and tailored to local regulations and market needs. Additionally, Siemens invested in virtual collaboration tools to enable remote learning and knowledge-sharing among its global teams.

Results:
Siemens improved the consistency and accessibility of its training programs across regions. Employees from different countries and time zones were able to access learning resources on-demand, increasing participation and knowledge transfer across borders. Siemens also saw an improvement in collaboration and innovation as global teams worked together on learning projects.

Creating Inclusive Learning Experiences for Global Teams

As organizations expand their reach across borders, it is essential to create learning experiences that are inclusive and reflect the diversity of the global workforce. This involves more than just translating training materials into different languages; it requires a commitment to understanding and respecting cultural differences.

1. **Cultural Sensitivity in Learning Content**

To ensure that learning content resonates with a global audience, organizations must consider the cultural norms, values, and expectations of their employees in different regions. This might involve adapting case studies to reflect local business practices, including culturally relevant examples, or even modifying communication styles to better align with regional preferences.

For example, a training program on leadership might emphasize different leadership qualities depending on the cultural context. In some cultures, hierarchy and authority may be more highly valued, while in others, collaboration and inclusivity may be prioritized.

2. **Supporting Diverse Learning Styles**

Just as individuals have different learning preferences, so do cultures. In some regions, employees may prefer direct instruction and formal learning environments, while others may thrive in more collaborative, hands-on learning experiences. Organizations need to offer a variety of learning methods to accommodate these differences, ensuring that all employees have the opportunity to learn in a way that suits them best.

3. **Addressing Digital Divide and Access Issues**

Not all regions have the same level of access to digital infrastructure. In some parts of the world, employees may face challenges related to internet connectivity, access to devices, or technological literacy. To create an inclusive learning environment, organizations must address these disparities by offering offline learning options, providing technology support, and ensuring that learning materials are accessible on a range of devices.

The Future of Global Learning and Remote Work

As remote work continues to gain traction and organizations expand globally, the need for effective, inclusive learning programs will only grow. In the future, we can expect even greater reliance on technology to bridge the gaps between regions, cultures, and time zones, while also offering more personalized and adaptive learning experiences.

Emerging trends such as **virtual reality (VR) training**, **augmented reality (AR)**, and **immersive simulations** will provide remote employees with highly engaging, hands-on learning experiences that feel as real as in-person training. AI will continue to enhance the personalization of learning paths, ensuring that employees across the globe receive the most relevant and impactful training.

Moreover, as global challenges such as climate change, social justice, and sustainability become more pressing, organizations will need to provide training that addresses these issues on a global scale, ensuring that employees are prepared to contribute to solutions that benefit society as a whole.

Conclusion: Embracing Global Learning in a Remote-First World

Learning beyond borders is no longer a distant goal—it's the reality of today's workplace. As organizations continue to operate across countries and cultures, and as remote work becomes more widespread, the need for effective, inclusive global learning programs has never been greater. By leveraging technology, fostering cross-cultural competence, and creating flexible, accessible learning experiences, organizations can empower their employees to thrive in a globalized, remote-first world.

In the final chapter, we'll look ahead to future trends in learning and development, and explore how organizations can prepare for the continued evolution of the workplace.

Endnotes

1. EMFD. (2019). *The Siemens Global Learning Campus.* 5 The Siemens global learning campus.pdf (globalfocusmagazine.com)

10 WHAT'S NEXT? FUTURE TRENDS IN WORKPLACE LEARNING

The workplace is evolving at a faster pace than ever before, driven by technological advancements, demographic shifts, and changing workforce expectations. As these transformations continue to shape the future of work, learning and development (L&D) must also adapt. The future of workplace learning will not be defined by static, one-size-fits-all programs, but by dynamic, personalized, and immersive experiences that empower employees to continuously grow and evolve.

In this chapter, we'll explore the most significant trends that are set to redefine workplace learning in the coming years. From the rise of artificial intelligence and immersive technologies to the growing importance of lifelong learning and adaptability, these trends will drive the next era of employee development.

1. Artificial Intelligence (AI) and Machine Learning: The Future of Personalization

As AI continues to advance, its role in workplace learning is becoming more sophisticated and impactful. **AI-powered learning platforms** are already providing personalized content recommendations, analyzing employee performance, and identifying skills gaps. But in the future, AI will go even further, offering hyper-personalized learning experiences that are tailored to each employee's unique needs, preferences, and career goals.

Predictive Learning Pathways

One of the most exciting developments in AI-driven learning is the concept of **predictive learning pathways**. These systems will analyze an employee's past performance, learning history, and even industry trends to predict what skills they'll need in the future. Based on this analysis, the platform will recommend training programs that align with both the employee's current role and future career trajectory. This will ensure that employees are always developing the skills needed for emerging challenges and opportunities.

For example, if AI detects that an employee is excelling in project management and leadership but may need more advanced technical skills as their role evolves, it will automatically recommend relevant courses, certifications, or even mentors to support their growth.

Real-Time Feedback and Adaptation

AI will also make real-time feedback and adaptation a standard part of the learning process. Instead of waiting for formal evaluations, employees will receive immediate, data-driven feedback on their progress. AI systems will adapt the learning experience based on this feedback, offering additional resources or adjusting the difficulty of tasks to ensure optimal learning outcomes.

This real-time adaptability will keep employees engaged and challenged at the right level, helping them build skills more effectively and efficiently.

2. Immersive Technologies: Virtual Reality (VR) and Augmented Reality (AR)

Immersive technologies like **virtual reality (VR)** and **augmented reality (AR)** are poised to revolutionize workplace learning by providing employees with hands-on, experiential learning opportunities in simulated environments. These technologies can recreate real-world scenarios, allowing employees to practice skills, make decisions, and solve problems in a risk-free setting.

Virtual Reality for Training

VR is already being used in industries like healthcare, manufacturing, and defense to train employees in complex procedures and high-stakes environments. In the future, we'll see VR expand into more industries, offering immersive training experiences for a wide range of roles—from customer service to leadership development.

For example, a manager might use VR to practice difficult conversations with employees or navigate complex team dynamics in a simulated environment. This hands-on approach allows learners to develop emotional intelligence, decision-making skills, and confidence without real-world consequences.

Augmented Reality for On-the-Job Learning

AR, on the other hand, overlays digital information onto the physical world, providing real-time guidance and support during tasks. AR will be particularly valuable for on-the-job learning, where employees can access step-by-step instructions, checklists, or videos as they complete tasks in real time.

For example, a technician might use AR glasses to receive instructions on how to repair a piece of equipment, with diagrams and prompts appearing in their field of vision. This just-in-time learning allows employees to build skills while performing their duties, reducing the need for separate, off-site training sessions.

One company that has successfully leveraged immersive technologies to enhance soft skills training is PwC. Here's how they used VR to drive impactful learning outcomes:

Case Study: PwC's Use of Virtual Reality (VR) for Soft Skills Training[1]

Overview:
PwC, one of the world's leading professional services firms, has been at the forefront of using emerging technologies in workplace learning. They sought a way to improve the soft skills of their employees—particularly in areas like leadership, communication, and empathy—using immersive learning techniques.

Solution:
PwC implemented virtual reality (VR) training as part of their **Digital Fitness App**, which offered employees immersive experiences to practice soft skills in realistic, simulated environments. The VR modules allowed employees to engage in scenarios such as negotiating with clients or leading difficult conversations, all in a risk-free setting.

Results:
PwC found that VR training was more effective at developing soft skills compared to traditional methods. Employees who completed the VR training showed improved confidence in handling real-world interactions and reported higher engagement with the learning process. PwC continues to expand its use of immersive technologies to enhance learning outcomes.

3. The Growth of Lifelong Learning and Microlearning

The days of completing formal education and relying on that knowledge for an entire career are over. As the pace of change accelerates, employees need to continually update their skills and knowledge. This is driving the shift toward **lifelong learning**—the idea that learning should be a continuous process that extends throughout an individual's career.

The Importance of Lifelong Learning

Lifelong learning is becoming essential as roles evolve and new technologies reshape industries. Employees must be able to reskill and upskill continuously to remain relevant in the workforce. Organizations that foster a culture of lifelong learning will be better equipped to adapt to change and innovation, while employees will feel empowered to take control of their career development.

Microlearning: Flexible and On-Demand

Microlearning—delivering content in small, focused units that can be consumed quickly—is also on the rise. This trend will continue to grow as employees seek flexible, on-demand learning that fits into their busy schedules. In the future, we'll see microlearning integrated even more seamlessly into daily workflows, with employees accessing bite-sized lessons, videos, or quizzes during brief moments of downtime.

For example, an employee might complete a 5-minute lesson on negotiation tactics while waiting for a meeting to start. By making learning accessible in small bursts, microlearning supports the continuous development needed to stay ahead in a fast-paced world.

4. Social and Collaborative Learning

Learning has always been a social activity, and as workplace structures become more collaborative, the need for social learning will continue to grow. Employees want to learn from their peers, share knowledge, and solve problems together. The future of workplace learning will place a greater emphasis on **collaborative learning platforms** that encourage interaction, discussion, and shared experiences.

Peer-to-Peer Learning and Mentorship

Peer-to-peer learning, where employees share insights and experiences with one another, will become a key part of workplace learning strategies. This informal, collaborative approach helps employees build relationships and learn from real-world expertise that may not be captured in formal training programs.

Mentorship will also play a more prominent role in learning and development, with organizations creating more structured programs that pair employees with mentors who can provide guidance and feedback. Digital platforms will support these relationships, enabling remote mentorship and virtual knowledge-sharing.

Collaborative Tools and Learning Communities

Collaborative tools like Slack, Microsoft Teams, or other enterprise social networks will facilitate learning communities where employees can ask questions, share resources, and work on projects together. These platforms will create a more interactive learning experience, where employees can learn in real time, problem-solve collaboratively, and share best practices.

For example, a sales team might use an online forum to discuss strategies, share new techniques, and provide feedback on customer interactions. These discussions, combined with formal learning content, help employees continuously improve and adapt to new challenges.

5. Data-Driven Learning: Measuring ROI and Impact

As organizations invest more in learning and development, the ability to measure the impact of these programs will become increasingly important. **Data-driven learning** will allow organizations to track the effectiveness of training initiatives and understand how learning translates into performance improvements and business outcomes.

Learning Analytics

Learning analytics—collecting and analyzing data on employee learning behaviours and performance—will become more sophisticated. Organizations will be able to measure not just how many employees completed a course, but how effectively the training improved skills, productivity, and engagement.

For example, a company might analyze the performance of employees who completed leadership training, comparing their progress to those who haven't yet participated. This data will help organizations refine their learning programs to maximize impact and ensure that employees are receiving the right training at the right time.

Personalized Learning Insights

Data-driven platforms will also offer personalized insights for employees, showing them how their learning aligns with their career goals and where they can improve. For example, an employee might receive a dashboard that tracks their progress toward mastering certain skills, along with recommendations for additional learning resources or stretch assignments.

This level of personalization helps employees stay engaged and motivated, as they can see tangible results from their learning efforts and understand how it contributes to their growth.

6. The Future Workforce: Adaptability and Resilience

As the workforce continues to evolve, the skills that employees need to succeed will also change. In addition to technical skills, **adaptability** and **resilience** will become increasingly important. The ability to learn, unlearn, and relearn in response to changing circumstances will be critical for employees and organizations alike.

Building a Resilient Workforce

To prepare for the future, organizations must focus on building a workforce that is not only skilled but also adaptable and resilient. This means fostering a **growth mindset**, where employees view challenges as opportunities for learning, and encouraging a culture of **continuous development**.

In the future, employees will need to be comfortable with ambiguity, able to pivot quickly, and open to acquiring new skills as their roles evolve. Organizations that prioritize adaptability and resilience will be better positioned to navigate the uncertainty of tomorrow's job market.

Preparing for the Gig Economy and Project-Based Work

The rise of the gig economy and project-based work will also impact workplace learning. As more employees take on short-term projects or freelance roles, organizations will need to offer flexible, on-demand learning that helps workers quickly acquire the skills they need for specific tasks or projects.

This shift will require a rethinking of traditional career development models, with learning paths becoming more fluid and adaptable to accommodate non-linear career trajectories.

Conclusion: Embracing the Future of Learning

The future of workplace learning is exciting, dynamic, and filled with opportunities for innovation. As technology continues to evolve, and as the workforce becomes more diverse and dispersed, organizations will need to embrace new learning models that are flexible, personalized, and driven by data.

By adopting these emerging trends—AI-powered learning platforms, immersive technologies, microlearning, social learning, and more—organizations can create a culture of continuous development that prepares employees for whatever the future holds. In this new world of work, the ability to learn and adapt quickly will be the key to success, for both employees and organizations alike.

Endnotes

1. Talespin. (2020). *Talespin Teams with PwC on VR Study Proving Efficacy of VR Soft Skills Training*. [Talespin Teams with PwC on VR Study Proving Efficacy of VR Soft Skills Training](#).

CONCLUSION: LEARNING TO LEAD THE FUTURE

As we move into an era defined by rapid technological advancement, shifting workforce dynamics, and an increasingly interconnected global economy, one thing is clear: learning will be at the heart of future success. Both organizations and individuals must embrace learning as a continuous, dynamic process that shapes the way we work, innovate, and lead. The ability to learn quickly, adapt to new realities, and reskill in response to change is no longer just a competitive advantage—it's a necessity.

This book has explored the many facets of modern workplace learning, from the rise of personalized learning journeys and the power of AI to the importance of building a culture of continuous development. As we look ahead, it is important to understand that learning is not only about acquiring new skills but also about fostering the right mindset—a mindset that views change as an opportunity, embraces challenges, and seeks growth at every turn.

Leading the Future Through Continuous Learning

In today's fast-paced environment, **leaders who champion continuous learning** will be the ones who guide their organizations through uncertainty and disruption. They understand that learning is no longer confined to classrooms or formal training sessions—it happens every day, in real time, through experiences, collaborations, and technology-driven platforms.

Leaders must prioritize creating an environment where employees are empowered to take charge of their own development. By providing the right tools, resources, and support, organizations can foster a culture where learning is embedded into the fabric of the workplace. When employees are equipped with the mindset and opportunities to grow, they become more agile, innovative, and ready to tackle the challenges of tomorrow.

Learning for Agility and Resilience

The future workforce will need to be more agile and resilient than ever before. Disruptions such as automation, AI, and global crises will continue to reshape industries, requiring employees to constantly reskill and adapt. The ability to pivot quickly, learn new skills on demand, and apply them in real-world scenarios will be critical to both individual and organizational success.

Reskilling and upskilling will play a pivotal role in this transition.

Organizations that invest in their employees' development, especially in high-demand skills like data analytics, digital fluency, and emotional intelligence, will build a future-ready workforce capable of navigating uncertainty. At the same time, employees must take responsibility for their own learning journeys, actively seeking out opportunities to enhance their skills and stay relevant in a rapidly evolving job market.

The Power of Technology in Learning

Technology will continue to transform the way we learn, offering more personalized, accessible, and engaging experiences than ever before. From AI-driven learning platforms that offer tailored content to immersive technologies like virtual reality that provide hands-on training, the future of learning will be powered by innovative tools that make continuous development easier and more effective.

Organizations must leverage these tools to create learning ecosystems that cater to the diverse needs of a global, remote, and digitally-savvy workforce. The combination of human creativity and technology will open new doors for how employees can grow, collaborate, and solve complex problems in real time.

Cultivating a Growth Mindset

At the core of successful learning is the **growth mindset**—the belief that abilities can be developed through dedication, effort, and continuous learning. Cultivating this mindset in employees and leaders alike will be the key to thriving in a future where change is the only constant.

A growth mindset encourages experimentation, learning from failure, and embracing challenges as opportunities for development. Organizations that foster this mindset will build a culture of resilience, where employees are not afraid to take risks, make mistakes, and grow from them. This culture will drive innovation, foster collaboration, and ensure that learning is viewed as an ongoing journey rather than a destination.

A Future-Ready Workforce

The future of work belongs to those who are ready to embrace change, learn continuously, and lead with vision and empathy. For organizations, this means reimagining traditional approaches to learning and development, creating personalized, adaptive learning experiences that prepare employees for the challenges ahead. For individuals, it means taking ownership of their own development, seeking out new opportunities for growth, and staying curious and open to new ideas.

In a world that is constantly evolving, the ability to learn will be the defining factor that separates those who thrive from those who struggle to keep up. As the workplace continues to change, those who lead with a commitment to learning—who prioritize growth, adaptability, and innovation—will shape the future of work and drive lasting success for themselves and their organizations.

Learning to Lead the Future

As we conclude this journey through the evolving landscape of workplace learning, it's clear that the future is filled with both challenges and opportunities. Those who embrace continuous learning, foster a culture of growth, and leverage the power of technology will be the leaders who guide their teams and organizations toward sustained success.

The future of work is not something that happens to us—it's something we actively create through our actions, decisions, and commitment to growth. By learning to lead the future, we take control of our destiny, ensuring that we are not only prepared for what lies ahead but empowered to shape it.

ABOUT THE AUTHOR

I'm Frederique Bergeron, an HR leader and author who's passionate about creating workplaces that prioritize people, flexibility, and innovation. Over the past 25 years, I've worked with organizations to navigate the challenges of modern work environments, helping them build cultures that are grounded in trust, empathy, and employee engagement.

As an advocate for remote and hybrid work, I've helped businesses implement flexible work models that benefit both employees and companies. My approach is shaped by years of experience in talent management, organizational development, and fostering employee well-being.

In my writing, I explore the intersection of technology, workforce trends, and human connection—offering practical strategies for thriving in an evolving world of work.

In **The Future of Learning at Work: How Technology, Neuroscience, and Personalization Will Shape the Workforce**, I delve into the critical role of continuous learning in preparing organizations for the future. I highlight how AI, neuroscience, and personalized learning can transform employee development, with real-world case studies to guide leaders and teams through this transformation.

www.ingramcontent.com/pod-product-compliance
Lightning Source LLC
Chambersburg PA
CBHW070409230526
45471CB00006B/2714